WHA
TAKE A J
ENGLAND'S HISTORY AND CULTURE.

WELCOME TO ENGLAND!

• Early Roman influence • William the Conqueror • King Henry VIII • Winston Churchill • Queen Elizabeth II • Buckingham Palace • Big Ben • The Tower of London • The London Underground 'Tube' • English Holidays and more!

KID PLANET BOOKS INCLUDE REAL-LIFE PICTURES AND STORIES TO HELP KIDS LEARN!

PERFECT FOR HOMESCHOOLING OR TEACHING!

@KIDPLANETCHILDRENSBOOKS

@KIDPLANETBOOKS

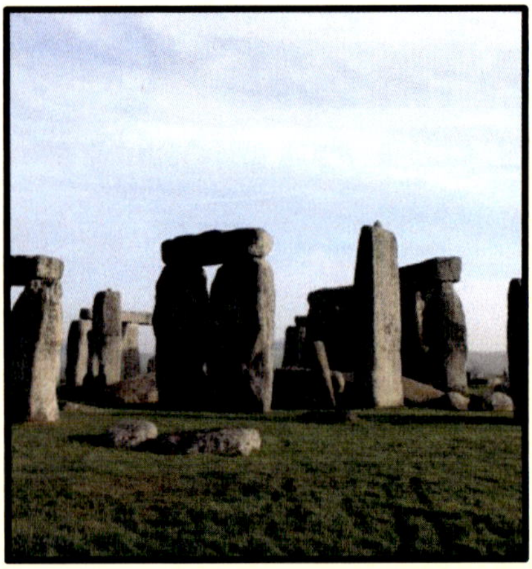
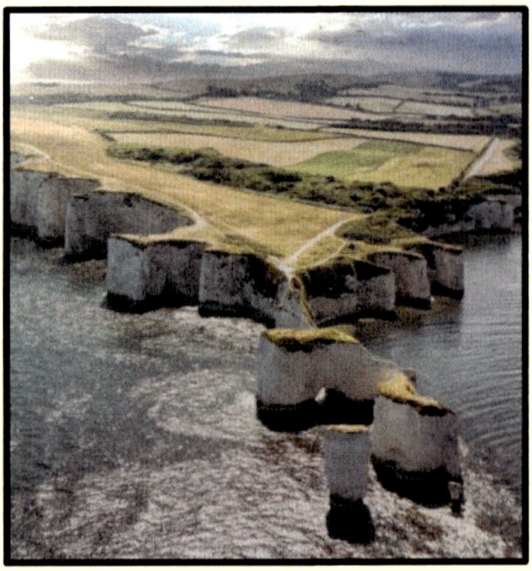
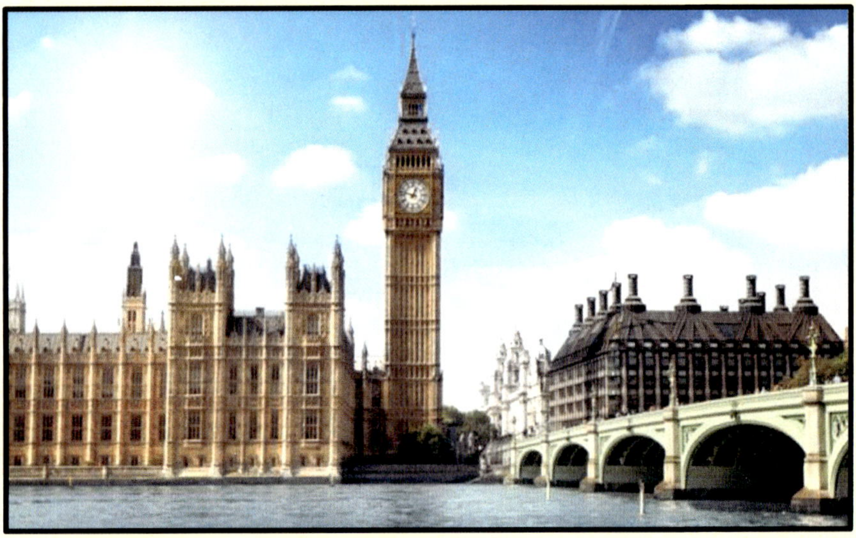
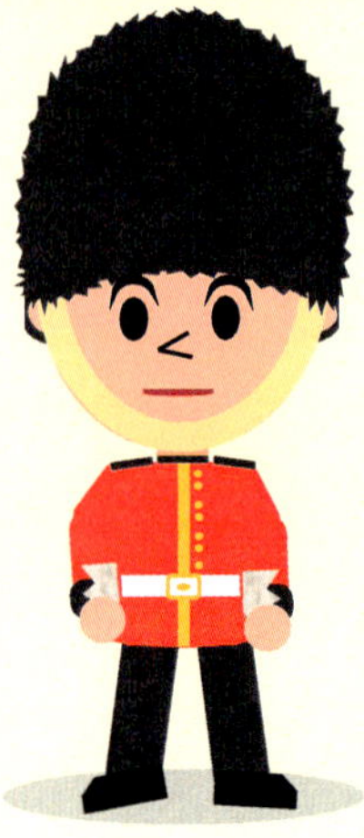
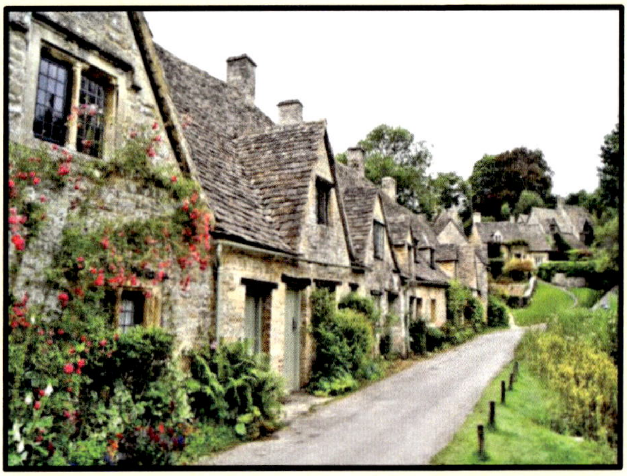

HELLO AND WELCOME TO KID PLANET, KID HISTORY! MY NAME IS OWEN!

Welcome to England! England is one of the most beautiful countries in the world and has some amazing places to visit!

England is a country that is rich in history. It's home to ancient monuments like Stonehenge and building marvels like Big Ben! We get around by using underground subways called the 'tube', and England is one of the last countries in the world to still have a queen!

Would you like learn more about my home country? I would love to take you on a tour to teach you all about it! Ready? Let's go!

LET'S LEARN ABOUT ENGLAND!

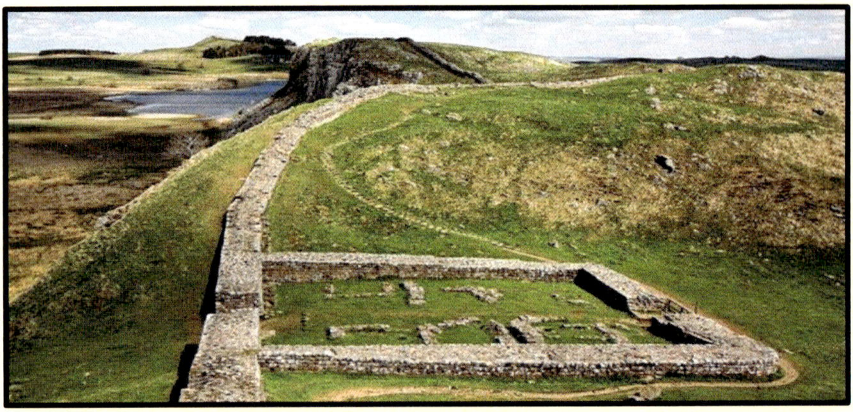

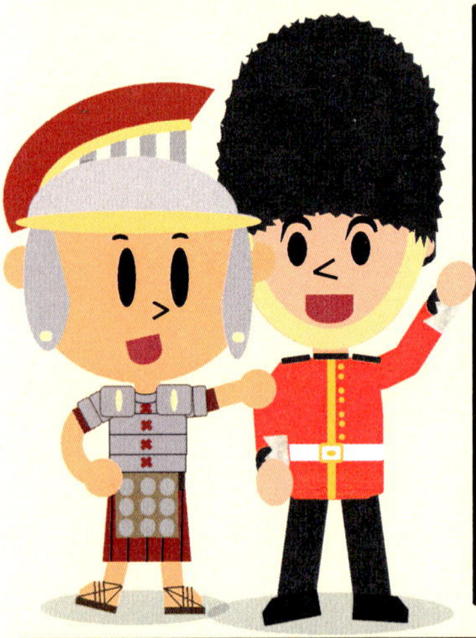

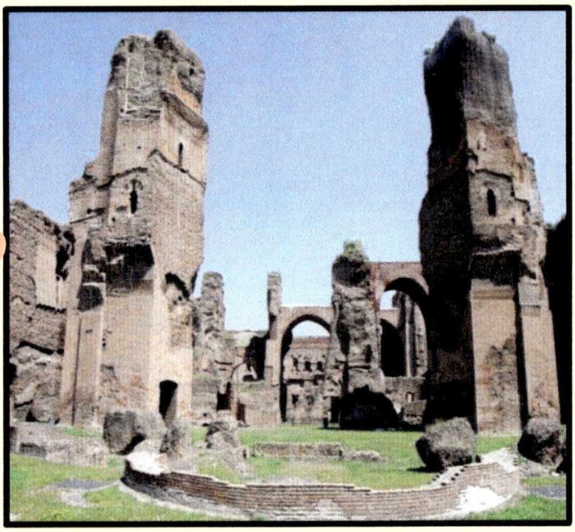

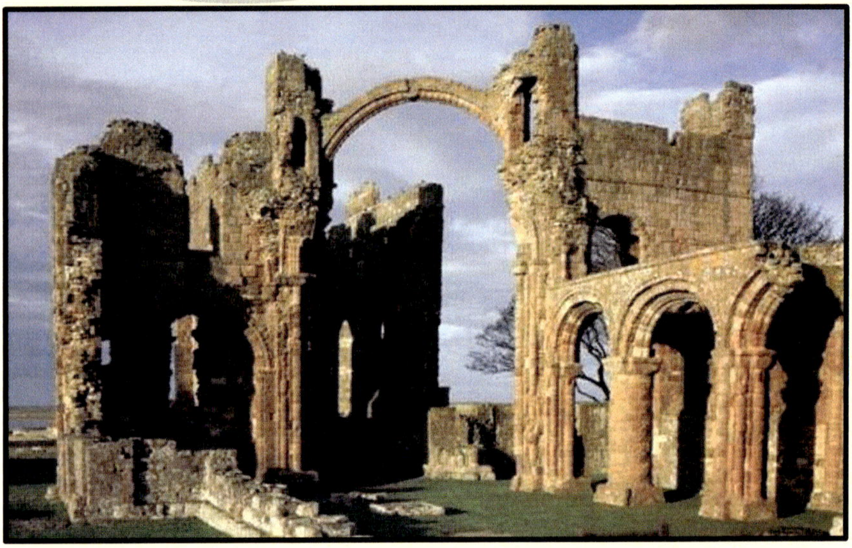

EARLY ROMAN INFLUENCE

One of the earliest inhabitants of England was the Roman Empire. The Romans lived on the island with another group called the Anglo Saxons. These were some of the England's earliest natives and were spread across the island. The Romans ruled over the native Anglo Saxons in which they had conquered in earlier battles.

The Romans were responsible for creating many early bridges, roads and towns in England or as it was called at the time, Britannia. The Romans founded many of England's most famous cities such as Manchester, London, York, Gloucester and Winchester. The ending of words that contain 'cester/chester' derive from the Roman Latin word for fort. Thus, cities like Manchester and Winchester have a meaning of 'Fort Man' and 'Fort Win'.

As time passed the Roman Empire grew too large. It became difficult for the Roman Empire to maintain its further territories and Britannia was extremely far away. Enter the Vikings or also known as the Danes. The Danes quickly conquered the remaining natives that were left over after the withdrawal of the Roman army. The Danes were able to establish their own government and began ruling the locals. However, the native Anglo Saxons were not as content being ruled by the Danes as they were being ruled by the Romans.

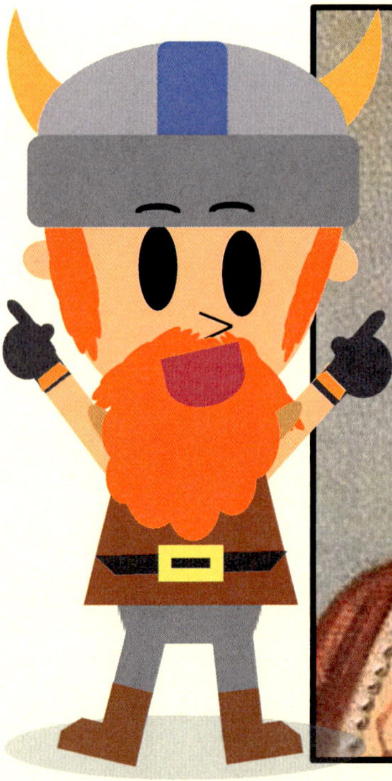
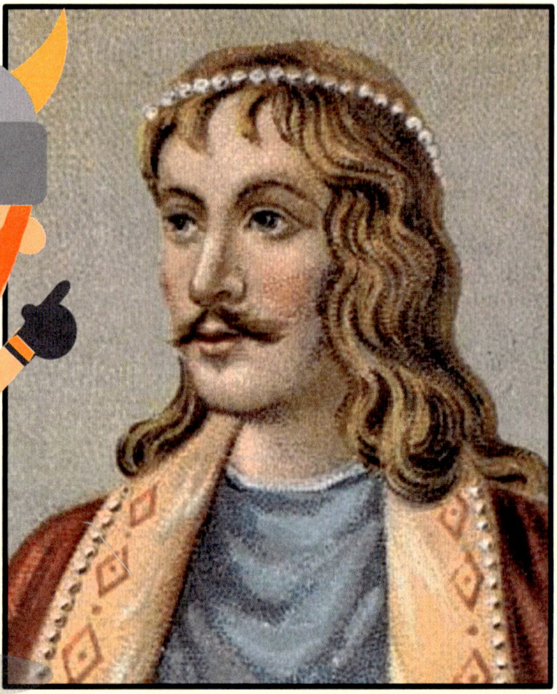
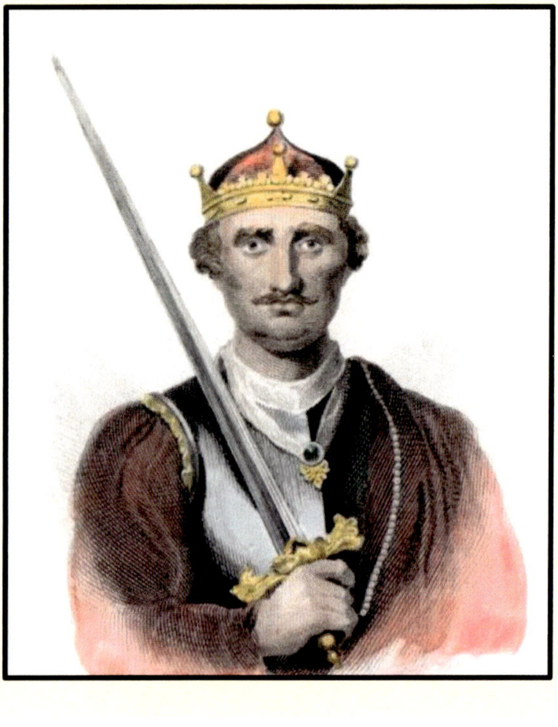
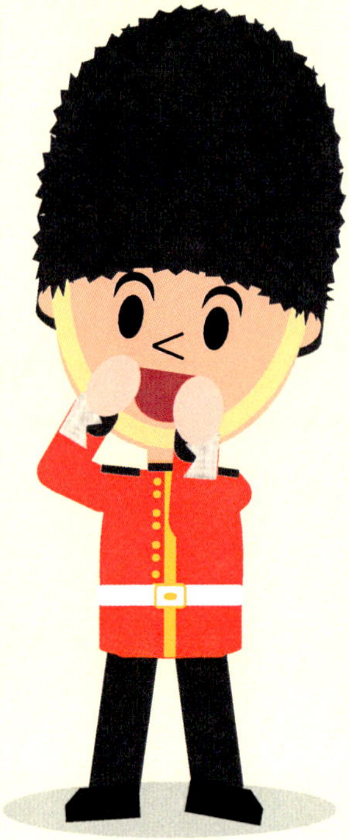

CANUTE & WILLIAM THE CONQUEROR

The English rebelled against the Danes and drove them out of Britannia. This made Canute the Great, King of the Danes, very mad. His father had conquered the Anglo Saxons just two years earlier and now they were rebelling again. He decided to conquer England himself.

Canute sent his strongest armies with a goal to conquer all of England. However, his main target was the city of London and King Edmund. It took numerous attempts to catch the king and defeat his armies, but eventually King Edmund surrendered. Edmund and Canute struck a deal to split ownership of England. Edmund would keep the territory south of the Thames River and Canute would control the north. However, Edmund died two weeks after the agreement due to unknown causes and Canute took over all of England.

A group of rebels called the Normans from a French town called Normandy were getting ready to attack England. The Normans were led by a man named William the Conqueror and they felt that their native English lands were stolen. William sailed his forces to England in an attempt to win their lands back. There was little that Canute and the Danes could do to stop William. He and his armies effectively took over all of England and he continued to rule England from that point on. William's lineage has stood the test of time as his descendants still sit on the throne of England today!

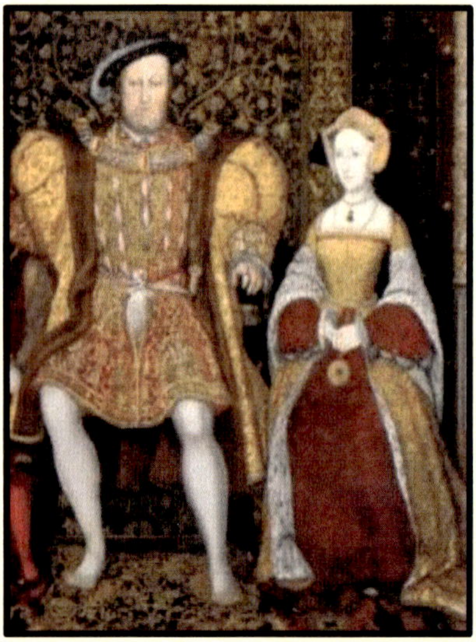
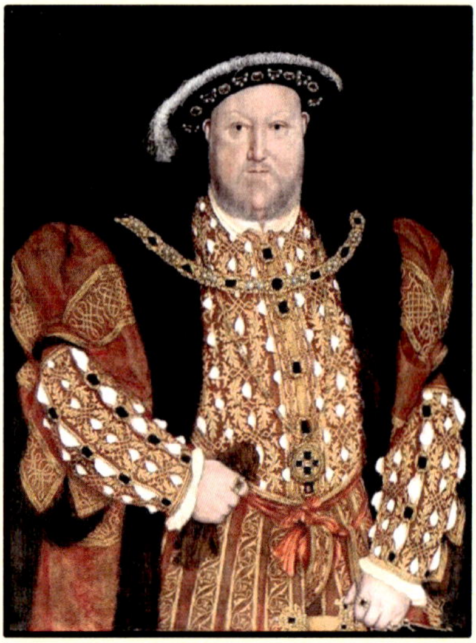
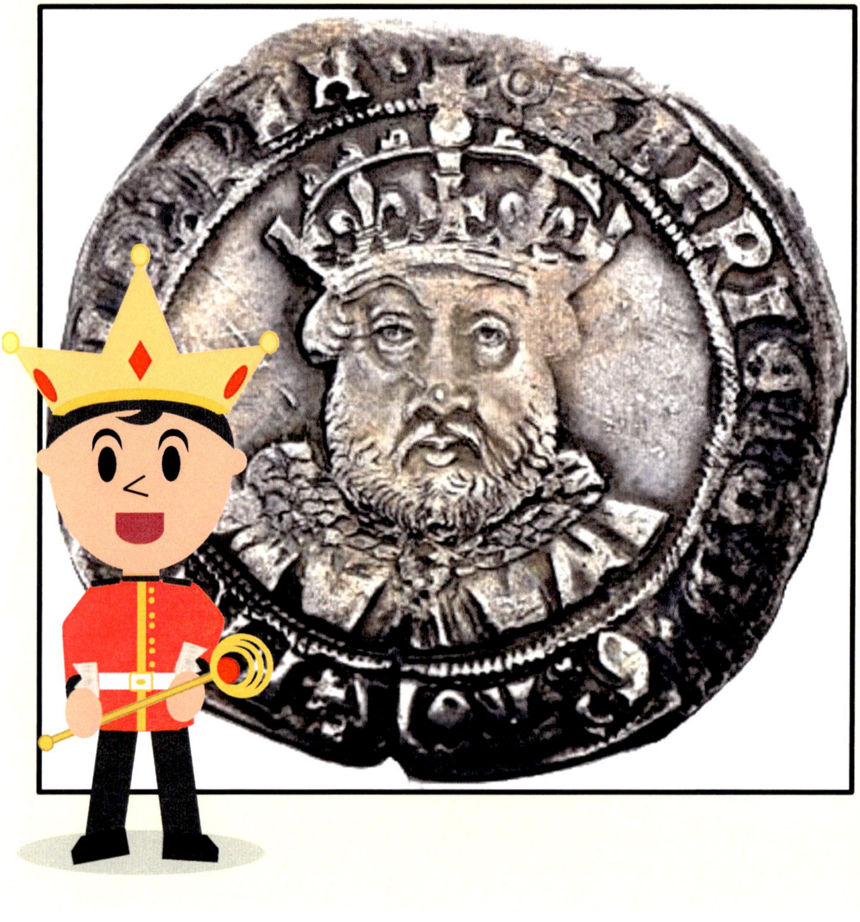

KING HENRY VIII

England went through numerous kings and queens after William the Conqueror passed. One of the most famous Kings in England's history was King Henry VIII. King Henry was known as one of the most selfish, ruthless and extravagant kings in all of England's history. King Henry was famous for many reasons but one of the most notorious stories of Henry is he had been married six different times. He was a key figure during a time called the 'Reformation'. During this time there were many changes taking place in in the world in the form of ideas, teachings, and religions.

Henry was a complex person. He was self-centered, loud, and careless. However, he was also smart, athletic and musical. The King was constantly angry that he was not able to bear a son to take control after he passed. King Henry VIII became vicious towards those near him, and he lost his control over the country.

A little-known fact about the King was that he hated being called 'old copper nose'. Henry was having trouble paying for his wars against Scotland and France. So, he advised the English coin printers to use less silver on the making of new coins in an effort to save money. The changes caused the coins to wear down on the front, and the image would fade to reveal the cheaper metal underneath. This was bad as Henry's face was on the coin and the wear left him with a shiny copper nose.

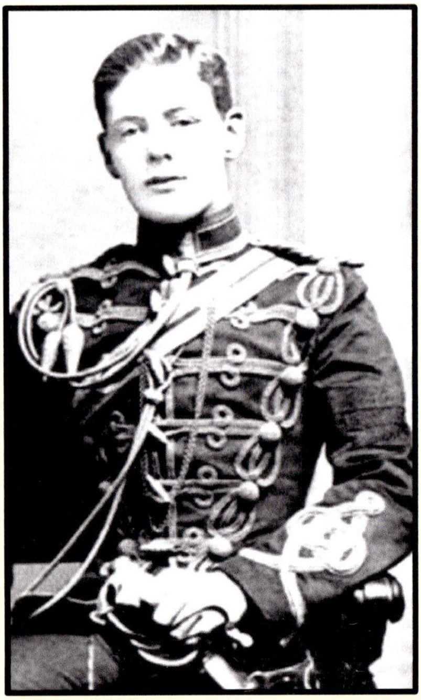
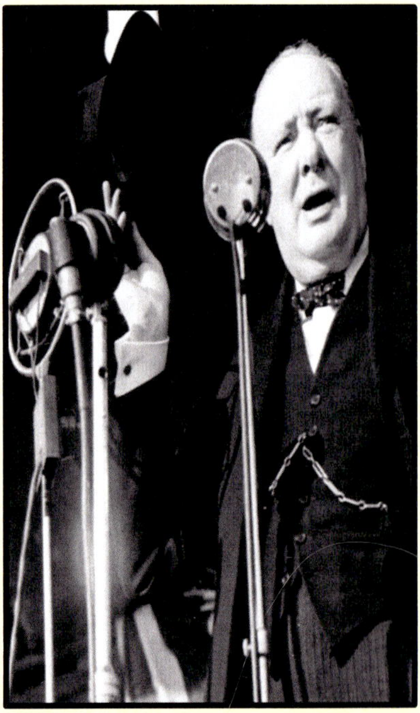
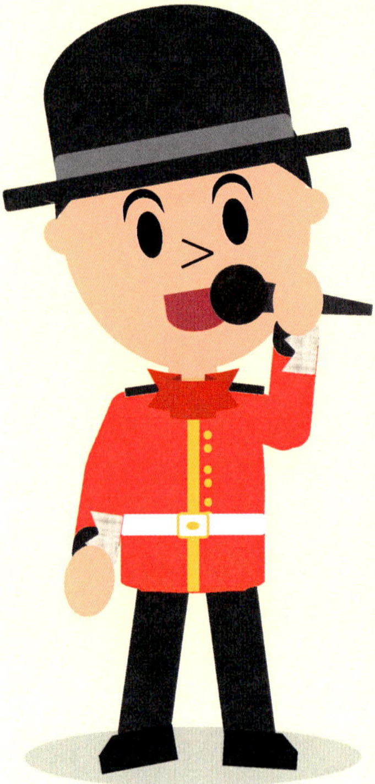
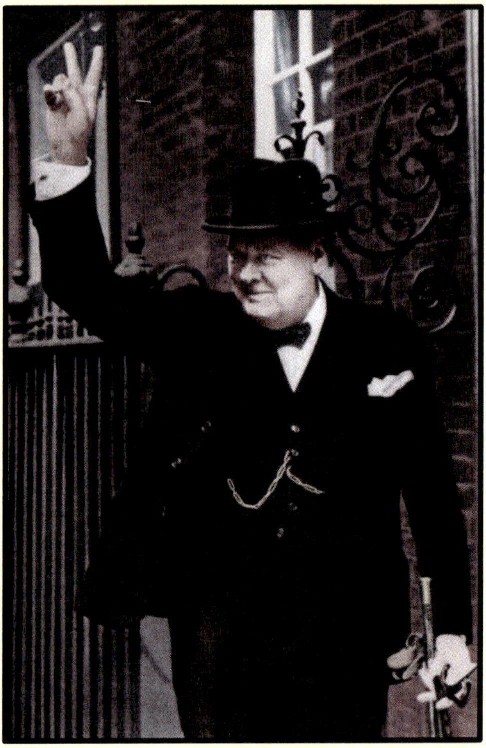

WINSTON CHURCHILL

Winston Churchill was Prime Minister of England and one of the world's greatest leaders. Churchill was born into a wealthy English family and his father was a prominent British politician. After graduating school, he attended a military academy and spent time traveling the world as a military journalist. He would write stories about England fighting in battles and would portray what was happening for those back home. It was during this time that he developed his superior public speaking skills.

In 1900, Winston began working as a politician in England's parliament. He worked in numerous positions in government and spent the next few decades learning how England's government operated. It was in 1940 that he became the Prime Minister of England after the previous leader, Neville Chamberlin, resigned. English citizens were worried about Adolf Hitler's army and wanted a strong leader like Churchill.

Churchill was able to lead the country through some of its most tumultuous times. His speeches during World War 2 helped motivate the troops and citizens when the outcome looked bleak. England and its allies were able to win World War 2 and Winston played a major part. He continued to serve in government and help guide England until his passing in 1965.

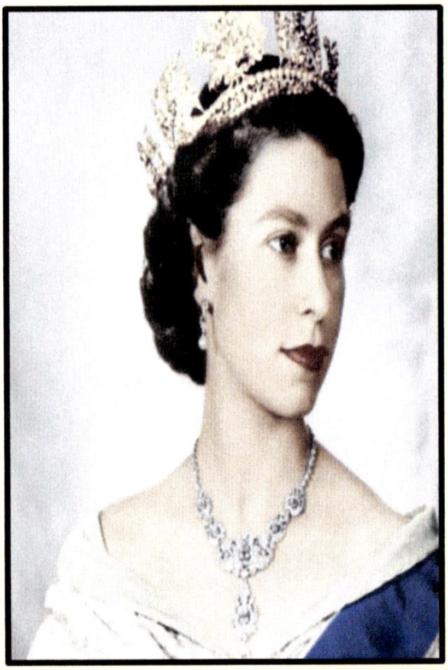

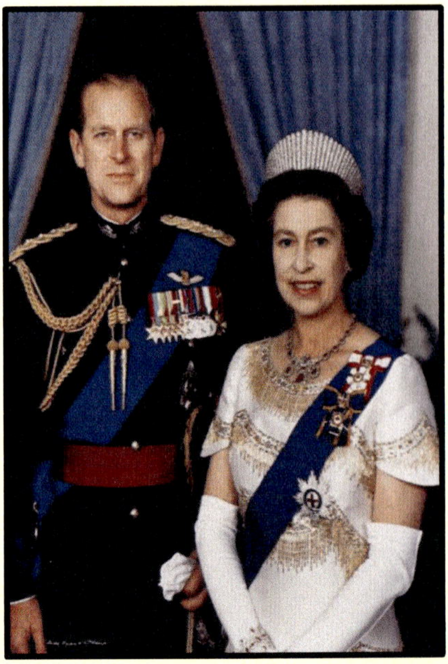

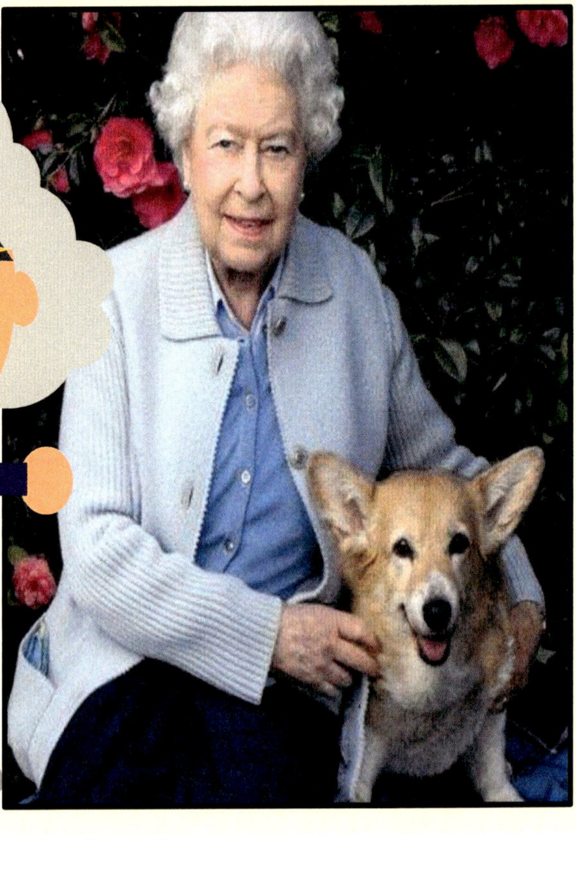

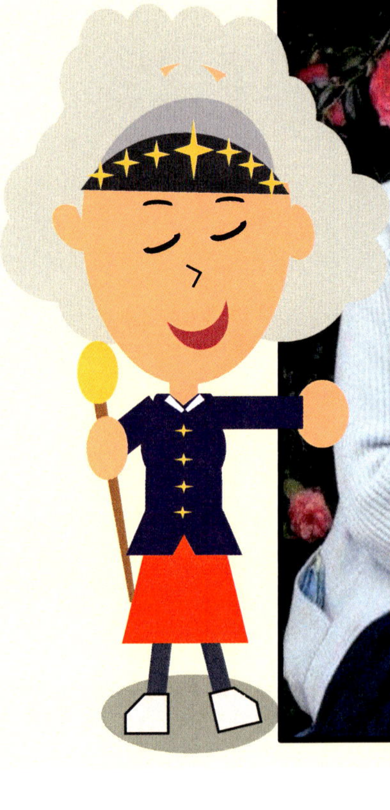

QUEEN ELIZABETH II

Queen Elizabeth II is the longest serving monarch in England's history. She was crowned in June of 1953 and is England's current monarch. She has been Queen through some of England's most memorable times. Queen Elizabeth has been a symbol of grace, strength, and dignity to not only the English people, but the whole world.

She was born into a royal family, but she was not considered to be in line to the throne. A series of events in her family took place in which ended with her father becoming the King of England. This meant that 10-year-old Elizabeth was next in line to rule England. After her father's passing, she became Queen and has held the title ever since. Elizabeth was married to Prince Phillip the Duke of Edinburg and together raised a large family. As time passed, the 'Windsor' family had become world famous, and they were treated like celebrities.

The Queen has lots of hobbies including pigeon racing and watching football. However, one of her favorite hobbies is spending time with her corgis. It is her favorite dog breed, and she has owned dozens. Queen Elizabeth has also been known to write numerous of Christmas cards over the years with the total being over fifty thousand! Finally, she loves technology. Queen Elizabeth has an Instagram account and even sent one of the first ever emails in 1976.

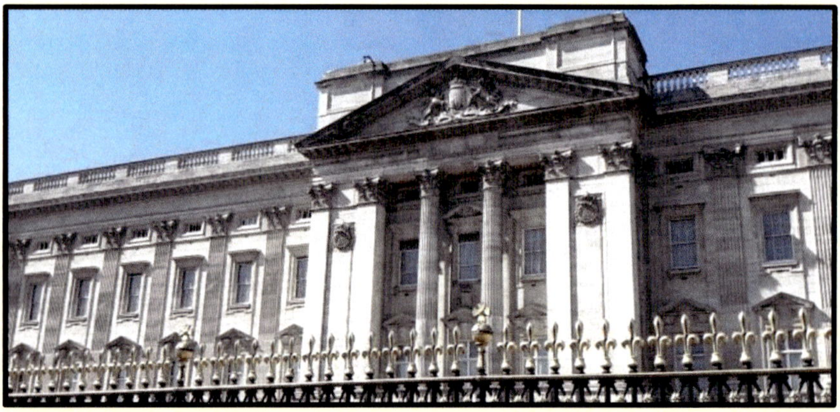

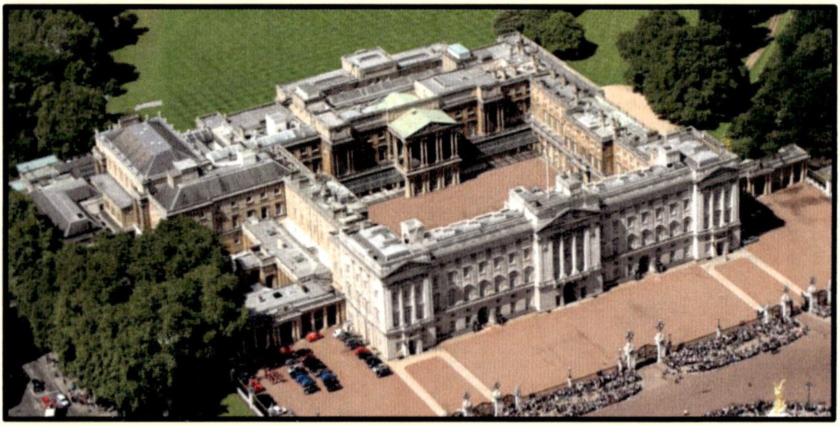

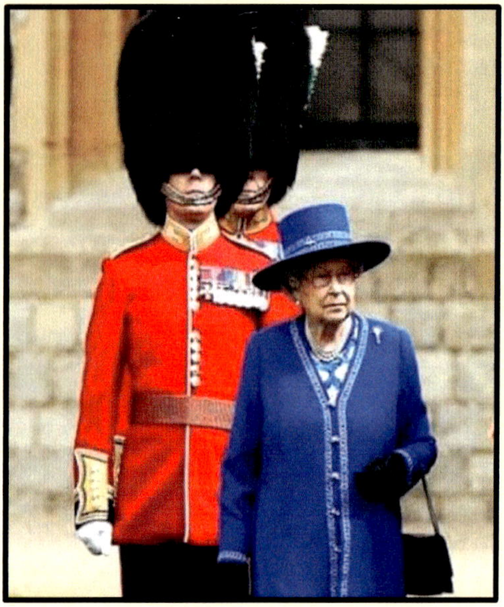

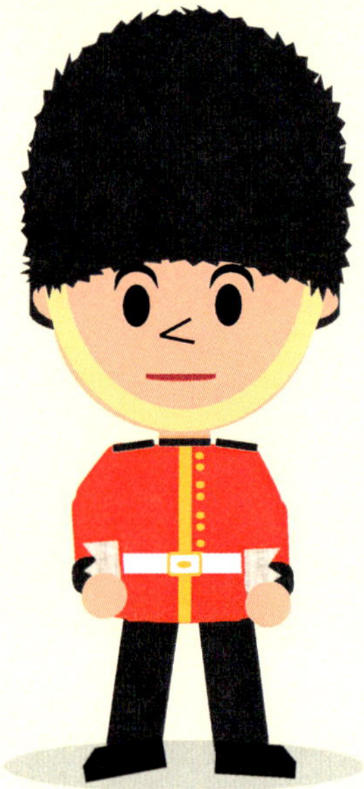

BUCKINGHAM PALACE

The Queen of England lives in a palace near London called Buckingham Palace. It was built in 1703 as a small home for the Duke of Buckingham. The home was purchased by the English royal family in 1761 when King George III acquired the home for Queen Charlotte. The Queen felt that the small home was not suitable for royalty, and she requested major expansions to make it look like it does today. Buckingham became the official royal residence to the Queen in 1837 when Queen Victoria made it her full-time home.

Queen Elizabeth II and her family have lived in the palace since 1952. The palace has more than enough space as it boasts more than 775 rooms! This includes 19 royal state rooms, more than 50 royal guest bedrooms, 188 staff bedrooms, and 78 bathrooms. The palace still plays an important part in the Queen's duties. The Queen uses the home to welcome many foreign leaders for diplomatic meetings and special events.

Buckingham Palace is where I work as a member of the Queen's guard. Our group is made up of soldiers from 5 different regions of Europe. We oversee protecting the Queen while she is at Buckingham Palace. We are world famous due to our unique uniforms with big bearskin hats. We are also known for staying at attention without moving. No smiling!

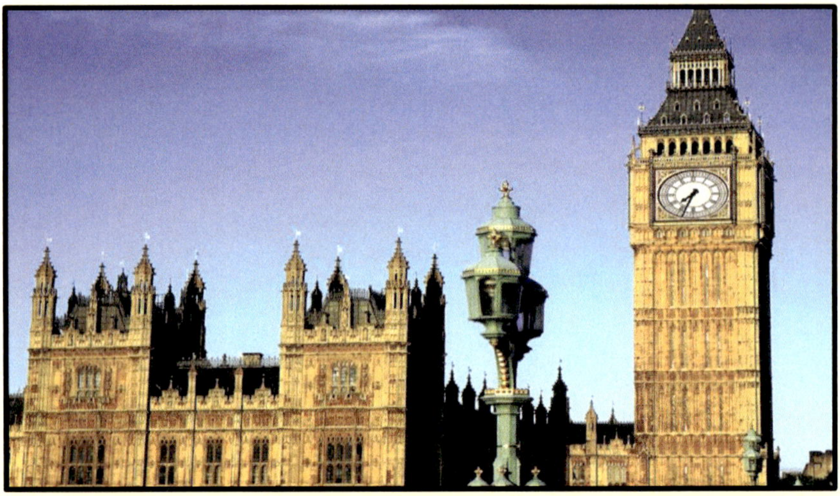

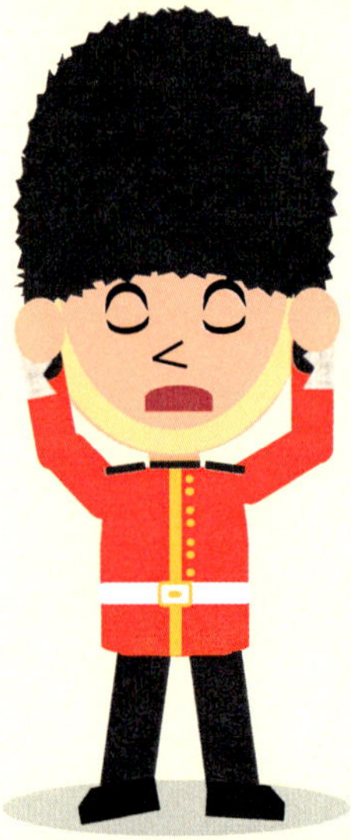

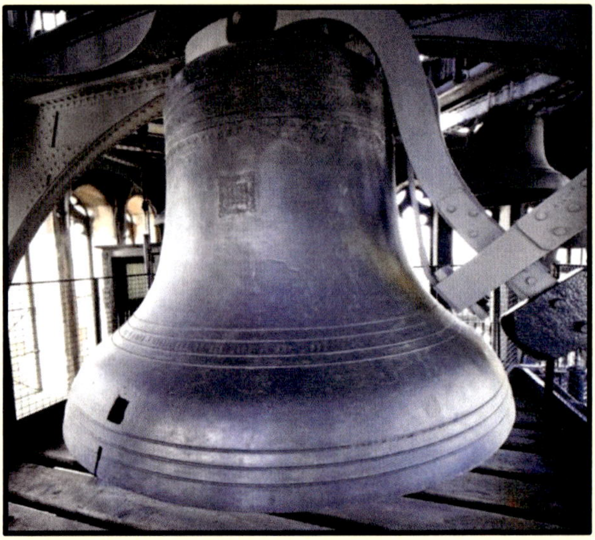

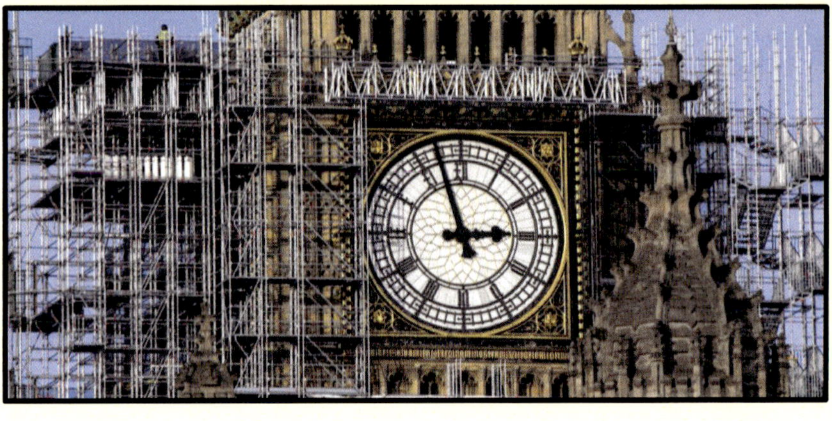

Big Ben

GONG! Yikes, what was that? Don't be startled. It's London's resident clock Big Ben. The name 'Big Ben' refers to the bell that resides inside of the tower. The tower has a total of five bells with Big Ben being the largest. The tower sits over 300 feet tall, and it was completed in 1859. It may sound surprising, but Big Ben is known to be one of the most accurate tower clocks in the world. The bells chime every fifteen minutes with Big Ben booming on the hour.

Big Ben was commissioned to be built in 1834 after a fire burned down most of the Palace of Westminster. Parliament passed a bill in 1844 to incorporate a large clocktower into the new building. The Big Ben hour bell was the largest ever cast in the United Kingdom at the time. It was over seven feet high and weighed over 10 tons. Big Ben was so heavy that it required over 15 horses to pull the bell from where it was made to the Palace of Westminster. It took several days to lift the bell to the top of the tower, and Big Ben rang out for the first time on May 31, 1859.

The clock tower was re-named 'Elizabeth Tower' during Queen Elizabeth's 60th Diamond Jubilee celebration. In 2017 Big Ben stopped chiming as the tower began undergoing a four-year restoration project. The project was delayed due to the COVID-19 pandemic and is on track to be completed in 2022.

ENTRY TO THE TRAITORS' GATE

THE TOWER OF LONDON

Remember William the Conqueror? Well after his battles to win England, he began to feel nervous of the locals rebelling. He had an idea to build a massive stone fortress in London to his assert his royal power. William built the castle on top of a hill near the Thames River so that it would dominate the London skyline. The Tower of London's construction took nearly two decades to build.

The Tower of London is extremely secure and well defended. As years passed, numerous royal members have used the tower in times of trouble to protect their possessions. It also protects the world-famous crown jewels. Up until the 1800's, it was here that many types of armor were made, tested and stored. The tower also controlled the supply of the England's money as all coins were made at the tower from the time of Edward I until 1810.

The tower also has a darker reputation. It was here that King Henry VI was killed during the War of Roses. The Tower of London became England's main prison during the Tudor age and those that were sent to the tower were assumed to be tortured or worse. It housed some of England's most famous prisoners such as Guy Fawkes and Lady Jane Grey. There are claims that the tower is haunted, and that Anne Boleyn walks the area. Look for the tower's resident ravens. It's been said if all the ravens leave the tower, the end of the crown is near.

PUBLIC SUBWAY
UNDERGROUND
PUBLIC SUBWAY

MIND THE GAP
MIND THE GAP

THE LONDON UNDERGROUND 'TUBE'

Mind the gap! This is the world-famous London Underground railway system or also known as 'the tube'. The subway system was created in 1863 and has been upgraded many times over the years. The tube started as one underground railway and today has eleven connected rail lines. It is used by over two million people per day and is one of the busiest metro systems in the world.

The trains on the tube may only travel short distances from station to station but, they drive over 100,000 miles per year total! That means that these trains can move lots of people and on average over 1 billion Underground trips are made each year. It's not just passengers that are plentiful, but also animals. Mice are very plentiful in the subway, and it's estimated that over half a million mice live in the subway tunnels! However, these mice are helpful to the environment as they eat bug and mosquitoes that live in the underground tunnels.

The tube tunnels even served as bunkers during World War II when London was being attacked by Germany. The London Blitz was a series of nightly bombing raids that were conducted by the Germans against England. People would escape to the tunnels when the air raid sirens would begin to sound. The tunnels even had 20 thousand bunk beds installed to allow citizens to rest safely. It's easy to see why the tube has such a strong connection with the people of England!

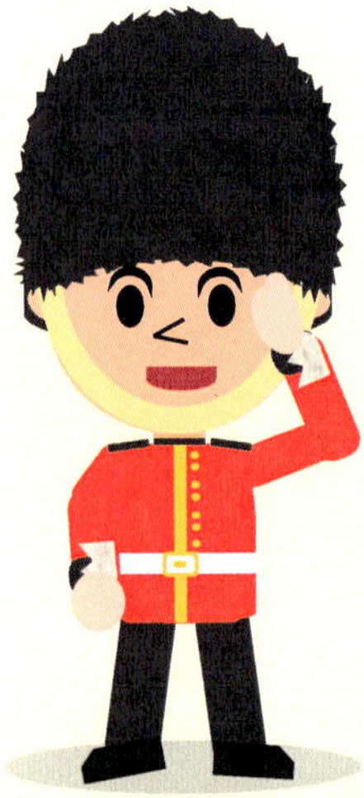

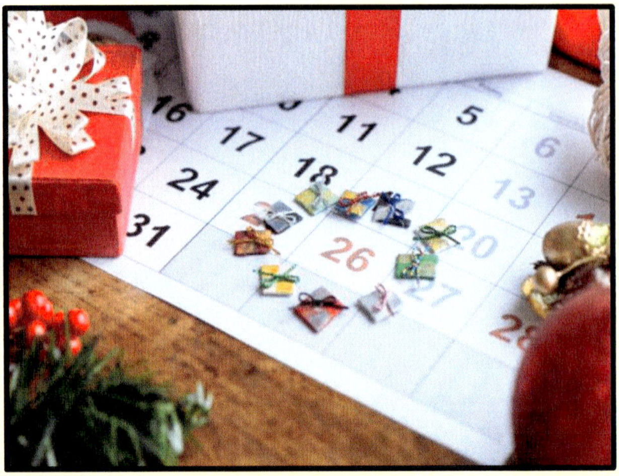

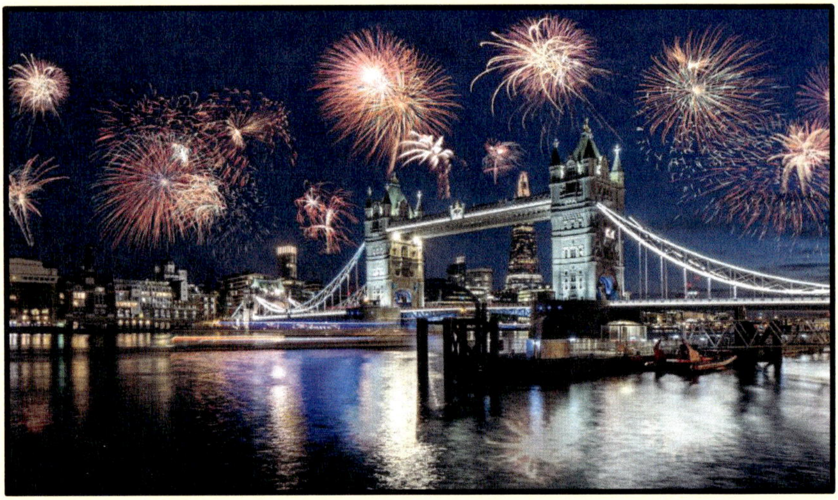

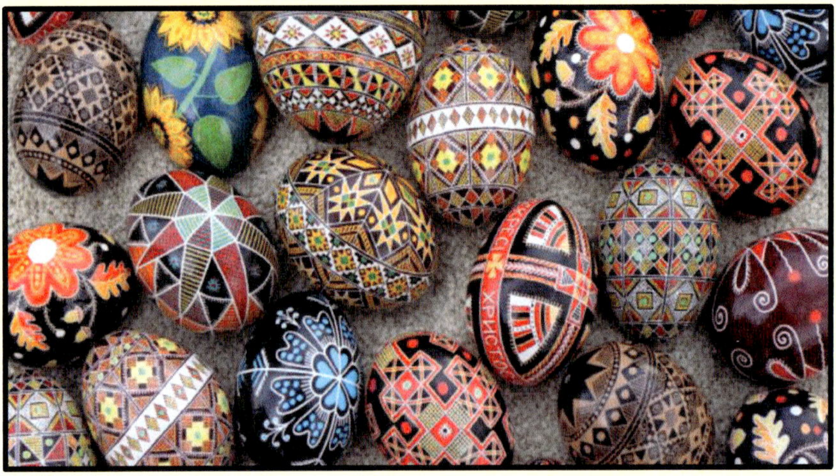

ENGLISH HOLIDAYS

    English citizens love to take time from their busy lives and enjoy a holiday. Boxing Day is celebrated each year on December 26th. Schools, workplaces and banks are closed to allow everyone to spend time with their loved ones. Boxing Day has been traced back in England for over 800 years. Scholars believe that the day was originally created for servants to receive gift boxes the day after the family they served celebrated on Christmas. Today, people in England spend Boxing Day with their family's eating food and watching sports.

    New Year's Eve and New Year's Day are another pair of festive holiday's that are celebrated by the English. New Years Eve is celebrated late in the evening of December 31st as the current year ends. People dance to music and attend large parties to celebrate the new year. The climax happens at midnight when the holiday changes to New Year's Day, which celebrates the official start of the new year. Midnight is even celebrated by Big Ben as the iconic tower is illuminated with lights and fireworks as it rings in the new year.

    Easter Monday is celebrated the Monday following the Easter holiday. Many businesses close for the day including banks and schools. Easter Monday originated during the medieval period in England when villages would hold celebrations or annual festivals. Citizens needed time to travel long distances and Easter Monday became a type of travel day after the events. Today, English families also use the day to travel home after visiting their friends and families.

REVIEW

- EARLY ROMANS
- WILLIAM THE CONQUEROR
- KING HENRY VIII
- WINSTON CHURCHILL
- QUEEN ELIZABETH II
- BUCKINGHAM PALACE
- BIG BEN
- TOWER OF LONDON
- LONDON 'TUBE'
- ENGLISH HOLIDAYS

LET'S REVIEW!

I hope you enjoyed learning about England. Let's review what we learned!

We found out about the influence that the Roman Empire had on England. After they left and the dust had settled, a man named William the Conqueror took control of the country.

King Henry VIII and Winston Churchill were very different people, but both were important to England's history.

Now you know that Queen Elizabeth II is the longest reigning monarch of England, and she resides in the 775 room Buckingham Palace.

If you happen to be in London, make sure to visit two of England's most iconic landmarks in the Tower of London and Big Ben!

Finally, we learned how English citizens travel by using the tube and all the wonderful holidays that celebrate.

UNTIL NEXT TIME...

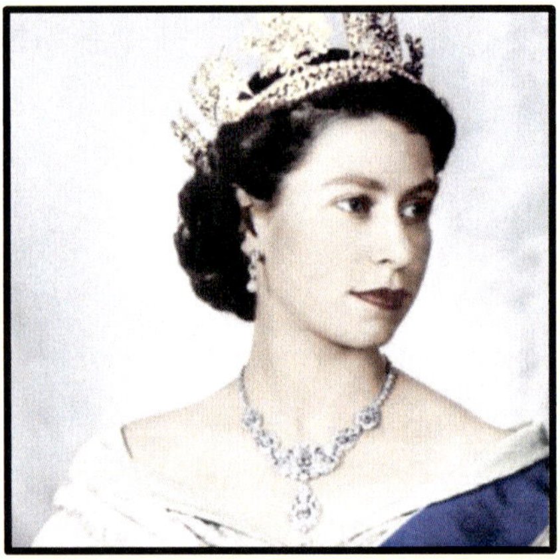

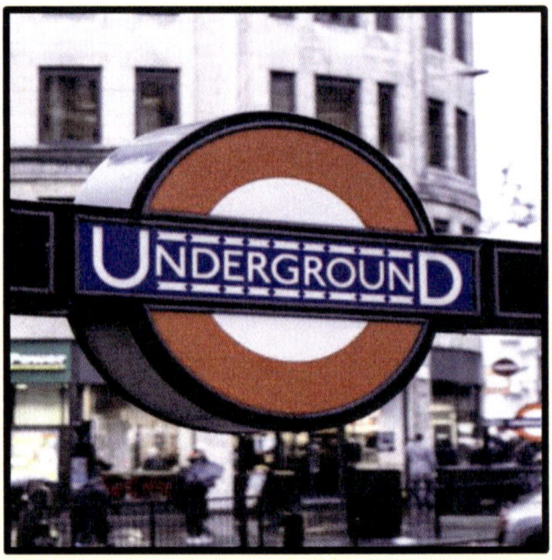
UNDERGROUND

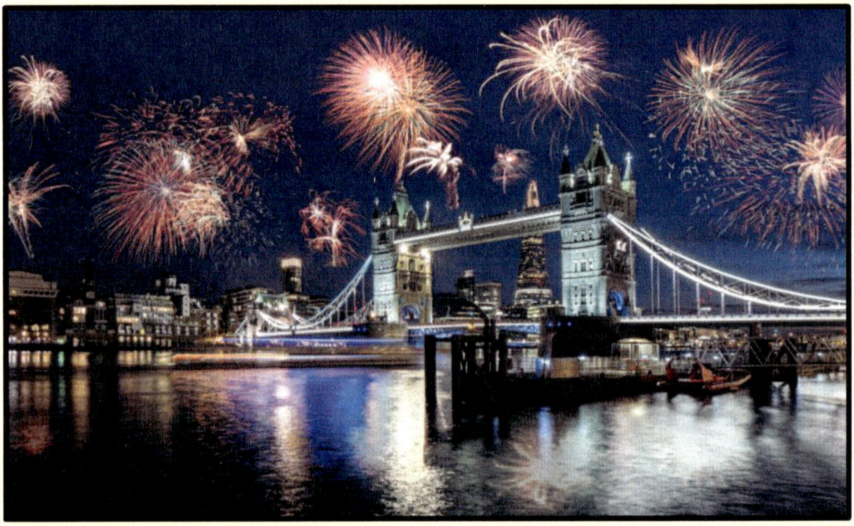

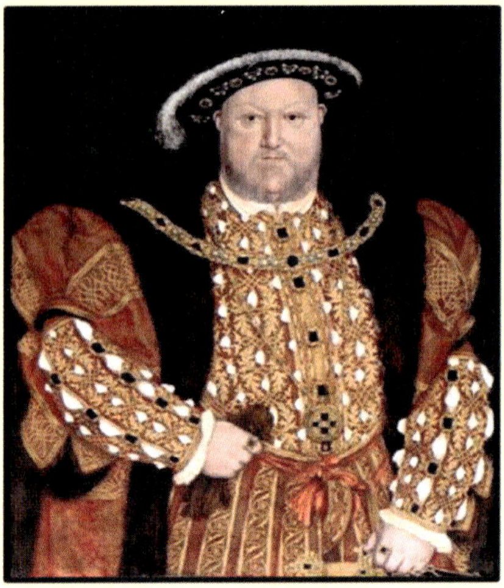

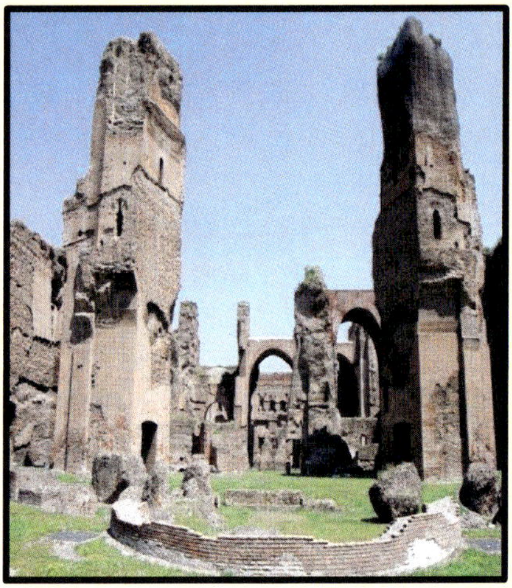

WELCOME TO ENGLAND!

CHECK OUT ALL OUR BOOKS!

Kid Planet Children's Books

TEACHING KIDS AROUND THE WORLD!

FOLLOW KID PLANET!
@KIDPLANETBOOKS

amazon.com/author/loganstover
facebook.com/kidplanetchildrensbooks